The Promise of Divine Restoration

The Promise of Divine Restoration

E.C. Nakeli

King's Word Publishing

© 2015 by E.C. Nakeli

Published by King's Word Publication

For your questions and publishing needs, write to:

> E.C. Nakeli
> 40 S Church st
> Westminster, MD 21157
> E-mail: *ecnakeli@yahoo.com*

Printed in the United States of America

All rights reserved. No part of this publication may be reproduced, stored in a retrieval systems, or transmitted in ay form or by any means— for example, electronic, photocopy, recording—without the prior written permission of the publisher. The only exception is brief quotations in printed reviews.

E.C. Nakeli

To contact the author, write to:

> E.C. Nakeli
> 40 S Church st
> Westminster, MD 21157
> E-mail: *ecnakeli@yahoo.com*l

The Promise of Divine Restoration / E.C. Nakeli

ISBN: 978-0-9850668-8-8

> Unless otherwise indicated, Scriptures references are from
> THE HOLY BIBLE, NEW INTERNATIONAL VERSION®, NIV®
> Copyright © 1973, 1978, 1984, 2011 by Biblica, Inc™
> Used by permission. All rights reserved worlwide.

Cover Design: Zach Essama -graphicspartner@gmail.com

Interior Design: Zach Essama -graphicspartner@gmail.com

Table of Contents

Dedication vii
Foreword ix
Introduction 1
Chapter 1: Understanding the Promise 5
Chapter 2: The Pathway to Divine Restoration 11
Chapter 3: The Promise of Divine Restoration 1 25
Chapter 4: The Promise of Divine Restoration 2 37
Chapter 5: The Promise of Divine Restoration 3 49
Chapter 6: The Promise of Divine Restoration 4 57
Chapter 7: A Case Study of Restoration – Naomi 63
Chapter 8: Pressing for Restoration: Putting God to Remembrance 79
Chapter 9: When God Remembers You 87
Conclusion 95

Dedication

To all those who are in need of restoration in any aspect of their life. As you read, may you find renewed hope to press on for total and complete restoration

Foreword

The Lord knows how and when to arrest our attention to fulfill His will. E. C. Nakeli could not initially understand the depths and benefit of restoration until God used his pastor to provoke something inside of him during a cross-over night in December 2009. The pastor declared that year to be a year of restoration; also, the outcome of this work to help many. I find it fascinating because it gives lots of hope to the hopeless; the down-trodden can rise again. It assures us that the battle is not yet lost. Restoration is beautiful. E. C. has written many books and this one is another tool for spiritual achievement in the hands of the reader. He is qualified to write because he has experienced restoration in the hands of the Master.

In this book, the author deals extensively on the different aspects of restoration such as restoration to God, restoration of the temple which is our body, restoration to His presence, restoration of the altar, restoration to worship and to service. You cannot read this book and remain unrestored. We find the convicting power of the Holy Spirit at work as we go through the pages of this book. Looking at the church today, we need to go back to the Lord and ask for fresh fire in order to tread the world in white! This book shows us the need to be restored and the blessings that follow. "*Whatever it is you have lost because of foolishness, and whatever it is you have not been able to experience because of ignorance the Lord is going to restore to you. Get ready to experience the things you have not experienced, and get ready to step into new territories of your inheritance in the Lord.*"

If you are spiritually dry, if you are not satisfied with the condition of the church and there is a cry for more spiritual experiences in your heart, then this book is for you. This book will spur you to get right with God and pray for revival. The church must return to the place of power and influence.

> Rev. Dr. Pius Forlu
> River of Life Center,
> Lanham, MD, U.S.A.

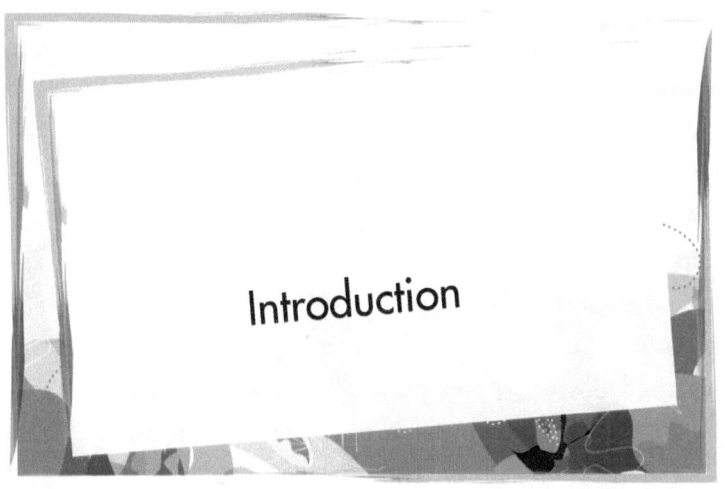

Introduction

On New Year's Eve of 2009, the Lord released a prophetic message to us in Christian Missionary Fellowship International, Kumba, Cameroon as we waited on the Lord after a session of prayer, praise and worship to close the year 2008 and enter the dawn of 2009 in the presence of the Lord.

As we waited on the Lord in silence as the second hand of the clock ticked for the crossing into another wonderful year of God's abundant grace, blessings, and favor, our senior pastor announced that 2009 was going to be a year of restoration. I can't describe to you the applause and rejoicing that filled the sanctuary as believers rejoiced and celebrated the word from above through His servant.

When I went home, by the Lord's leading, I was able to research what the Bible says about restoration. I wanted to understand the full scope of what God had spoken to us, so I armed myself with my Bible study tools to research God's promise of restoration. As I immersed myself in the word and searched diligently and prayerfully, I was stunned by what God has to say to us as far as restoration is concerned.

The next Sunday was going to be a joined service during which all the centers of the church come together for common fellowship. During the week when my senior pastor asked me to minister to the saints on Sunday, I then understood that God wanted me to teach the whole congregation on the vastness of His promise to us for the New Year. Until this day, I personally consider that message one of the best messages I have preached or taught as a minister of the gospel within the last twelve years or more that I've preached the word in different settings.

In this book, I am going to share with you the discoveries I made from the word during the period of research, what the Lord has taught me in addition to that on the topic of divine

Introduction

restoration, and my experiences of how the sovereign Lord has brought restoration to my own life.

In this book, we are going to answer the following questions: What is restoration? What is God's promise for restoration? What are the different domains of restoration? What are the pathways to restoration? And, who qualifies for restoration? I believe as we answer these questions in the light of God's word and under the anointing of the Spirit of the living God, you will come to see and understand what the Lord has in store for you as far as restoration is concerned. You will see and understand how you can enter into your own season of restoration and make your dwelling on Restoration Avenue in this life. God has promised restoration but you must understand that restoration will not just come to you unless you follow the principles that guarantee restoration.

May the Lord bless you and bring unprecedented restoration in every domain of your life that needs it, and may you become an instrument of restoration as you help others by your understanding, to enter into their full restoration.

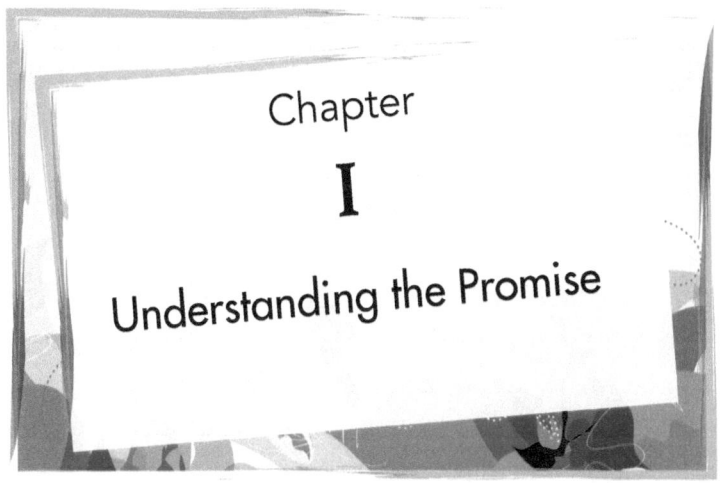

Chapter I

Understanding the Promise

What is Restoration?

Many of us have yet to come to even a partial understanding of the scope of the promise of divine restoration. Yes we have used the word often, and it seems to me the too much use of the word has hackneyed the word making it trite and common place. Therefore each time the word is used it fails to convey the true and total meaning of the sense in which the Lord has used it.

It seems to me our English translation of the words used in the Bible to convey the meaning of restoration fails to measure up to the Hebrew and Greek words used in the Bible. In the English Language the use of the word restoration means to bring back to an original state, condition, use, or position. It gives us the idea of what used to be but now it's not, at least the way it used to be. However the words used in the Bible go far beyond what our English language conveys.

As I studied the words translated as restoration or to restore in the Bible, I discovered some very intriguing meaning such as to be whole, sound, safe, complete, to turn about, to be lifted up, to perfect, to spring up, to mend, strengthen, repair, to make one what he ought to be etc.

The promise of divine restoration is vast beyond our wildest comprehension, yet it is true and within our grasped even if we may just understand only a glimpse of its entirety. When God promises restoration, He doesn't have in mind only the things that once were ours but which now are not for one reason or the other, but He also has in mind the things that were supposed to be ours which we never received either because of ignorance or foolishness.

The things that were meant to be yours but which were diverted by evil forces, God will give back to you. The things which you once owned or experienced but lost as a result of sin and compromise, God is about to restore to you. The things that you lost because of indulgence and laziness, God will restore to you. It doesn't matter how far removed you are from what you were or are supposed to be, once you understand the extend of the promised divine restoration and the pathway to receiving and experiencing it, nothing will be able to stop you as you set your heart on entering the divine promise.

The Extent of the Promised Divine Restoration

In a few lines, let me share with you the extent of the promised divine restoration. Once you have a glimpse of its extent, then you will be able to receive the most out of the promise, and why not all you ought?

Full restoration

In his second letter written to the church in Corinth the Apostle Paul said, *"9 We are glad whenever we are weak but you are strong; and our prayer is that you may be fully restored…11 Finally, brothers and sisters, rejoice! Strive for full restoration…"* (2Co 13: 9,11)

Paul prayed for them that they would experience full restoration because he had an understanding of the extent of divine restoration. He asked them to "strive for full restoration" because he knew that restoration has to be contended for so there was need to strive for it. So, for there to be restoration, you have to do your utmost, go all-out for it, and do your best. There is a part for you to play for there to be full restoration in your life. We will discuss this in details in a later chapter.

Again, Paul asked them to strive for full restoration because he understood that there could be partial or incomplete restoration. And it seems to me many of us in the modern-day church have settled for partial or incomplete restoration because we do not want to strive or worse still, because we do not know how to strive for full restoration. My hope is that by the time we come to the end of this study on the Promise of Divine Restoration, you will have complete knowledge, not only of the extent of this restoration but how to strive for it and experience it.

Double Restoration

"...even now I announce that I will restore twice as much to you." (Zechariah 9:12b)

The Father doesn't just want to restore to you fully all that you need restoration in but He has promised to restore twice as much to you. God is out for double restoration of that which you had or were, and that which you were supposed to have

Understanding the Promise

and be. That is 200% of all that is yours coming back to you from the God of restoration. From your relationships, fortunes, gifts and talents, health and wholeness, blessings etc.

God wants to bring back double into your life. That is the extent of divine restoration. All what God created you to be but which the circumstances of live seem to have robbed you of, God says He will make you what you ought to be, give you what you ought to have if you would strive for full and double restoration.

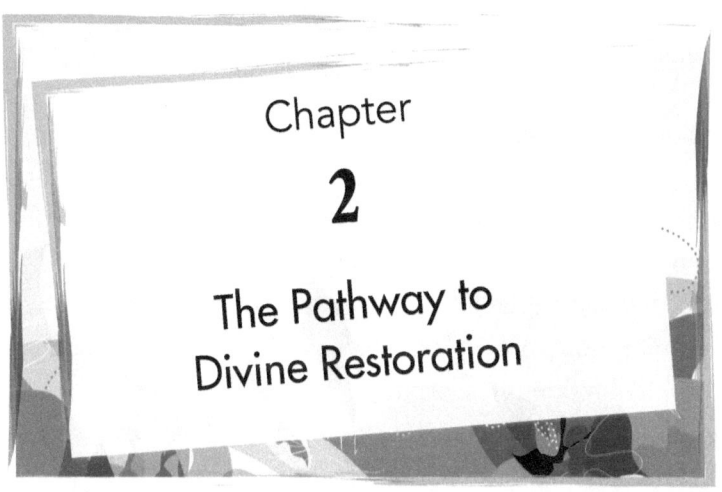

Chapter 2

The Pathway to Divine Restoration

One of the main reasons we as Christians fail to benefit from all that Christ accomplished for us is because we fail to understand how we are supposed to get that which is rightfully ours. To get to anyway or into anything, you must know the path to it before you take the decision to follow that path and stay on it until you get into what the path was leading you to. So briefly, I want us to look at ways by which God has established for us to receive our full restoration.

Understand Your Role

To enter full restoration, you must first understand the role you must play. Like every other blessing in the New Testament dispensation, Christ Jesus has made the price for you to be restored and for everything you lost to be restored to you, but there is a role you have to play to realize the blessing of restoration. In the verse we looked at earlier, Paul told the brethren in Corinth, *"⁹We are glad whenever we are weak but you are strong; and our prayer is that you may be fully restored…¹¹Finally, brothers and sisters, rejoice! Strive for full restoration…"* (2Corinthians 13:9,11a). So, to experience restoration, there's got to be:

1. Prayer

Paul said, they were praying for the Corinthians to be fully restored. It means that prayer is an aspect we must embrace on the path to restoration. Restoration will not just come looking for you. You will have to pray restoration into your life. Throughout the Psalms we find constant prayers for restoration lifted up to God:

> *"Restore us, Lord God Almighty; make your face shine on us, that we may be saved."*
>
> (Psalm 80:18)

The Pathway to Divine Restoration 13

> *"Restore us again, God our Savior, and put away your displeasure toward us." (Psalm 85:4)*
> *"Restore our fortunes, Lord, like streams in the Negev."*
> (Psalm 126:4)

So for you to enter restoration, you have to pray specifically for what aspects you are expecting God to bring restoration into your life.

2. Rejoicing

The second aspect on this pathway to restoration is to rejoice. After Paul told them he was praying for them to be fully restored, he now asked them to rejoice. The word used for rejoice here also mean delight. So Paul was telling them to delight in restoration. For restoration to come to you, you must delight in it. You must want it earnestly and rejoice over it as though you already received it. In other words you should celebrate restoration. That which you celebrate will come to you.

3. Striving

Next, he told them to strive (struggle, go all-out, make every attempt, do your best, endeavor, do your utmost) for full restoration. He was asking them to leave no stone unturned in their efforts to experience full restoration.

There are many forces out there which are bent on seeing you deprived of the very things Christ Jesus paid for you to receive and enjoy. To overcome them you have to strive. It should be more than just a careful wish for restoration. It should be more than mere talk. David had to make a relentless pursuit of the enemy to fully recover all what had been stolen from him. Though tired, exhausted, discouraged, and weary, he was determined to gain back what was rightfully his. Paul was telling the Corinthians, they too must be determined in order to experience full restoration.

4. Returning

"Return to the stronghold, O prisoners who have the hope; this very day I am declaring that I will restore double to you."

(Zechariah 9:12, NASB)

I want you to note that the same Hebrew word translated as restore in this verse is the same Hebrew word translated as return in the same verse. So, the Lord is asking you to restore yourself to the stronghold, the fortress as a step towards restoration. Many of believers have strayed from the word of God which should be a fortress for them. They have walked away from Bible principles and thereby lost the covering that was supposed to be theirs. Because they lost a covering over them, they have become prisoners to one form of bondage or another. They have lost the very things that were rightfully theirs. So for restoration to come to them, they must begin by returning to the Lord who is the stronghold of their life. They must return to the word of God and stick to it.

For restoration to come to you there must be a turning around in your life from every path that strays from divinely ordained principles. Once you return, you place yourself in a position for restoration to locate you. Do you have to do some returning? Are you in need to make a turn around? Then please do. You have to restore yourself to the stronghold of the unfailing word of God.

5. Expectation

> *"Return to the stronghold, O prisoners who have the hope; this very day I am declaring that I will restore double to you."*
> (Zechariah 9:12, NASB)

The Lord uses a definite article *"the"* to qualify the word hope in this verse. The same word translated as hope here could also mean expectation. No matter the prison in which you find yourself at this time, God says if you have the expectation for restoration, He will restore to you double. To enter full restoration you will have to expect it. It shouldn't just be a wish; you should be filled with expectations for restoration. Look forward to it with joy and delight. There is power in your expectations to bring you restoration; double, full, restoration.

6. Repentance

One of the main reasons why restoration has eluded many people in spite of their relentless pursuit of it is because they have failed to repent of the sins and compromises that brought about the loss in the first place. God cannot be mocked, God cannot be deceived.

If there is sin in your life, you need to get rid of it before you can expect full restoration. God will not restore to you only for the devil to deprive you of the restoration because of sin in your life. God is never wasteful of His resources. Repentance is a vital element for complete restoration. If this lacking, then all you do will be child's play!

It is written in the Book that:

> *5 "If you would seek God*
> *And implore the compassion of the Almighty,*
> *6 If you are pure and upright,*
> *Surely now He would rouse Himself for you*
> *And restore your righteous estate.*

⁷ "Though your beginning was insignificant,
Yet your end will increase greatly."

(Job 8:5-7, NASB)

²¹ "Yield now and be at peace with Him;
Thereby good will come to you.
²² "Please receive instruction from His mouth
And establish His words in your heart.
²³ "If you return to the Almighty, you will be restored;
If you remove unrighteousness far from your tent,
²⁴ And place your gold in the dust,
And the gold of Ophir among the stones of the brooks,
²⁵ Then the Almighty will be your gold
And choice silver to you.
²⁶ "For then you will delight in the Almighty
And lift up your face to God.
²⁷ "You will pray to Him, and He will hear you;
And you will pay your vows.
²⁸ "You will also decree a thing, and it will be established for you;
And light will shine on your ways.
²⁹ "When you are cast down, you will speak with confidence,
And the humble person He will save.
³⁰ "He will deliver one who is not innocent,
And he will be delivered through the cleanness of your hands."

(Job 22:21-30, NASB)

In both passages above the key condition is repentance. When there is repentance, then there will be restoration and all other things will fall in place. The issue with believers is that they go for the pursuit of the benefits of restoration while neglecting the very path that should lead then to restoration. It's like someone in Maryland who wants to go to New York but decides to take the path that leads to Florida. That individual can pray all he wants to and look as intently as possible, he will not meet any sign pointing to New York unless there is a complete turnaround to the right direction. Repentance is like your takeoff point to restoration. You cannot ignore or neglect this vital and most determinant aspect on the path to divine restoration.

7. Surrender

To drive home this point of surrender, I want us to look at what happened to king Nebuchadnezzar and how is it that he was restored.

> *"26 The command to leave the stump of the tree with its roots means that your kingdom will be restored to you when you acknowledge that Heaven rules. 27 Therefore, Your Majesty, be pleased to accept my advice: Renounce your sins by doing what is right, and your wickedness by*

being kind to the oppressed. It may be that then your prosperity will continue. "

²⁸ All this happened to King Nebuchadnezzar. ²⁹ Twelve months later, as the king was walking on the roof of the royal palace of Babylon, ³⁰ he said, "Is not this the great Babylon I have built as the royal residence, by my mighty power and for the glory of my majesty?"

³¹ Even as the words were on his lips, a voice came from heaven, "This is what is decreed for you, King Nebuchadnezzar: Your royal authority has been taken from you. ³² You will be driven away from people and will live with the wild animals; you will eat grass like the ox. Seven times will pass by for you until you acknowledge that the Most High is sovereign over all kingdoms on earth and gives them to anyone he wishes."

³³ Immediately what had been said about Nebuchadnezzar was fulfilled. He was driven away from people and ate grass like the ox. His body was drenched with the dew of heaven until his hair grew like the feathers of an eagle and his nails like the claws of a bird.

³⁴ At the end of that time, I, Nebuchadnezzar, raised my eyes toward heaven, and my sanity was restored. Then I praised the Most High; I honored and glorified him who lives forever.

His dominion is an eternal dominion;
his kingdom endures from generation to generation.

> *35 All the peoples of the earth*
> *are regarded as nothing.*
> *He does as he pleases*
> *with the powers of heaven*
> *and the peoples of the earth.*
> *No one can hold back his hand*
> *or say to him: "What have you done?"*
> *36 At the same time that my sanity was restored, my honor and splendor were returned to me for the glory of my kingdom. My advisers and nobles sought me out, and I was restored to my throne and became even greater than before."*

(Daniel 4:26-36)

Nebuchadnezzar had come to the point where he thought he was almighty and the Lord decided to humble him using a very severe method. The condition that was given him for his restoration to take place was that he should acknowledge the sovereignty of God, renounce his sins and do what was right. When he resisted Daniel's advice all what was decreed against him was fulfilled. He was dethroned and ostracized. He lived like an animal and reasoned like a beast, until he surrendered to the Lord and acknowledge His sovereignty.

There are many people living in rebellion against the Lord and yet are yearning for restoration. They have refused to acknowledge the supremacy, centrality, and sovereignty of the

Lord Jesus over several aspects of their lives. They have failed to surrender totally to the Lordship of Christ in every domain of their lives, yet such people are the ones praying and expecting restoration. You cannot enter total and complete restoration if there are aspects of your life not total submitted to the Lordship of the Christ Jesus. You must bring everything of yours in total and absolute surrender to Him, then will restoration come to you.

8. Connections

Another aspect on the pathway to divine restoration is tapping on the power of connections. In my book, *"The Power of Connections"* I talked of the fact that your connections in life will bring you uncommon restoration. Our example here was the Shunnamite who had travelled to a foreign land to settle there because of the famine that came on Israel (see 2 Kings 8). After a period of more than seven years she decided to return to her country.

On returning she realized she had lost everything and decided to go ask for her land and property from the king. As she arrived the king was talking with Gehazi, the servant of the prophet Elisha about the exploits of the man of God. And it so happened that the very time she stepped in Gehazi was talking about her. This lady had gotten herself connected to the prophet Elisha through her gifts and services to him. And because Elisha had influence in the courts of the king, her connection to him caused the king to ask that all what she owned before she left the land be restored totally to her.

This is the account of the story: *"⁵ Just as Gehazi was telling the king how Elisha had restored the dead to life, the woman whose son Elisha had brought back to life came to appeal to the king for her house and land. Gehazi said, "This is the woman, my lord the king, and this is her son whom Elisha restored to life." ⁶ The king asked the woman about it, and she told him. Then he assigned an official to her case and said to him, "Give back everything that belonged to her, including all the income from her land from the day she left the country until now."* (2 Kings 8:5-6)

This is what we term uncommon restoration. If you establish the right connections with the right people in your everyday life, at the right time, the Lord will use the power of your connections to bring about the necessary restoration in your life.

9. Command of faith

This is the aspect of restoration most believers try to use all the time. On its own, the command of faith will not bring you restoration unless it is used in sync with the other aspects of the path to divine restoration. This aspect should be used when you are sure that repentance, returning, surrendering, expectation, prayer, determination, and rejoicing are already in place, if not you will be wasting your time. The basis of the command of faith is the fact that the word says when a thief is caught he must restore what he stole.

> *"If anyone gives a neighbor silver or goods for safekeeping and they are stolen from the neighbor's house, the thief, if caught, must pay back double."*
>
> (Exodus 22:7)

> *"^{30} People do not despise a thief if he steals*
> *to satisfy his hunger when he is starving.*
> *^{31} Yet if he is caught, he must pay sevenfold,*
> *though it costs him all the wealth of his house."*
>
> (Proverbs 6:31)

And you and I know who the thief is; his name is satan the devil. Command him to restore the things he stole from you because of your ignorance, sin, or compromise. Command him to restore at least double. If I were you I would command him to restore sevenfold what he has stolen from my life.

If you employ the points we have treated above collectively and in sync with each other, there is no way full restoration will not be your portion. Now that we have seen the path to restoration, let us look at the promise of restoration in the next couple chapters.

Chapter 3

The Promise of Divine Restoration 1

Restoration to God

The first and foremost aspect of the promise of divine restoration is restoration to God Himself. The Lord Jesus came to restore to man the relationship he had with the eternal creator Elohim in the Garden of Eden. Ours is supposed to be a relationship of continuous fellowship and communion with the God of heaven.

The truth is many believers are not into a relationship with God. They are into Christianity for the blessings that come with it rather than the relationship it puts us into. Blessings are supposed to be by-products of our romance with divinity. Intimacy with divinity puts us in a place of enjoyment of the blessing of salvation. When we relate with God as we ought, we live contented and satisfied lives.

Is your relationship with God what it is supposed to be? Are you walking in unhindered fellowship and communion with your God? Is there room for improvement in that relationship? If there is any room for improvement, which I believe there should be, then you need restoration to God.

Remember we said at the beginning that restoration is not limited to what you used to be or what you used to have but goes further to what is supposed to or ought to be. So when we talk of your restoration to God Himself, we are not assuming that you have backslidden. What we mean is that no matter how advanced you are in that relationship, it's not what it's supposed to be yet, hence the need for restoration.

It is true that many people seeking restoration for one thing or another are living in total neglect of the cultivation of their relationship with God. They seek restoration from a God they do not know or whom they ignore in their daily choices and values. You can't experience full restoration unless you first seek to be restored to God.

Three times in Psalm 80, the Psalmist Asaph made this prayer, *"Restore us, O God Almighty; make your face shine on us, that we may be saved."* (Vv 3,7,19) in Psalm 85:4, the sons of Korah prayed, *"Restore us again, God our Savior, and put away your displeasure toward us."* and in Lamentations 5:21, the prophet Jeremiah prayed, *"Restore us to yourself, Lord, that we may return; renew our days as of old"*.

When God restores you to Himself, then He is restoring you to His favor, He is restoring you to His salvation, and to His pleasure. This is one aspect of restoration you have to pursue, restoration to God. When this takes place, every other restoration will be much easier. But when this is out of place, every other restoration cannot take place effectively. Full restoration begins with restoration to God.

Begin to ask God to restore you to Himself. Ask earnestly, fervently, persistently, and expectantly. Ask to feel the heartbeat of God. That is the place of intimacy with divinity. Decide that nothing will come between you and God.

Restoration to His presence

Next you need to be restored to God's presence. The presence of your heavenly Father has to be your home. Once that relationship is restored, then let His presence fill and permeate your whole life and being. You must come to the place where you are conscious of His presence in you, on you, around you, with you and for you. It is this consciousness of the divine presence that makes the believer invincible.

God wants to fill you with himself so that you become His presence wherever you find yourself. Restoration to His presence means you have easy access into the presence of God, with the privilege of bringing that presence to others and carrying others into His presence.

The prophet Hosea said, *"Come, let us return to the Lord… on the third day he will restore us, that we may live in his presence"* (Hosea 6:1-2). God wants to restore you to His presence that you may live there. When you live in God's presence it means everywhere you go and in everything you do, God's manifest presence will be with you.

You become a portal to the divine presence. It is the presence of God that empowers, emboldens, and anoints for triumph. When you get restored to His presence, you will feel at home with Him in prayer, meditation, Bible reading, and worship. You will be in no hurry whatsoever.

Restoration of the Temple

The Bible says your body is the temple of the Holy Spirit: *"Do you not know that your bodies are temples of the Holy Spirit, who is in you, whom you have received from God? You are not your own"* (1 Corinthians 6:19)

The truth is that for many of us we have lived in total neglect of the temple of God which is our bodies. The temple lies in shambles. We have exposed His temple to unclean things and opened the gates wide for the entrance of idols and other abominable things. We have erected idols in God's temple. It is time you restored the Temple which is your body. Like Josiah, you must rise up to purge the Temple of God, which is your body, of all that is there illegally. Overthrow the idols and purify the temple.

> *"The king and Jehoiada gave it to those who carried out the work required for the temple of the Lord. They hired masons and carpenters to restore the Lord's temple, and also workers in iron and bronze to repair the temple."*
>
> (2 Chronicles 24:12)

My dear friend, restore the temple so that God's presence and glory will dwell there abundantly for the blessing of everything you touch or come in contact with. Dethrone every idol erected in the holy place of your heart and let Christ alone be enthroned therein. If any part of your body is broken, asked the Lord to send His heavenly carpenters and masons to restore and rebuild the temple which is your body. No part of the temple should be in disarray or in disrepair.

Is there any part of your body which needs to be mended? There are specialists the King can send to help put things together. But first you must purge the temple of all unclean things and be committed to keep it clean and consecrated for the Lord's use and habitation.

Restoration of the Altar

When we started this study on The Promise of Divine restoration, I said there are things you have to do on your part in order that the Lord may fulfill His part to bring total and complete restoration. We saw part of your responsibility when we looked at the pathway to restoration in the previous chapter.

As we have looked at the first couple of aspects of the promise of restoration, we have also seen what role you have to play in being restored to God, His presence, and the need to restore His temple. Now let's talk about the need to restore the altar.

The purpose of the temple is the altar of prayer, praise, worship and sacrifice. For many people, their problem is a result of the fact that the altar in their temple is in ruins. Fallen or dilapidated altar is the cause for many problems for which people are in need for restoration. During the time of Israel's backsliding and eventual bondage, after Josiah restored the temple, the next thing he did was to restore the altar of the Lord.

The Bible says of Manasseh, that, *"15 He got rid of the foreign gods and removed the image from the temple of the Lord, as well as all the altars he had built on the temple hill and in Jerusalem; and he threw them out of the city. 16 Then he restored the altar of the Lord and sacrificed fellowship offerings and thank offerings on it, and told Judah to serve the Lord, the God of Israel." (2Chronicles 33:15-16)*

We talked about getting rid of the idols and purifying the temple in the previous point. Once that is taken care of you will be able to restore the altar in your life. You cannot restore the altar if the temple is not restored. And that is the mistake many people make. They try to restore the altar of praise and worship, prayer and sacrifice when the temple of their lives is in shambles and desecrated by idols which have been enthrone there for one reason or another. Recently the Lord began to speak to me about the gods of this land which many people are worshipping.

I was preparing a message for our congregation on the topic, God's Solution to Adversity. As I prepared my message from *Judges 6*, when I came to verse 10 the Lord told me there is the reason for the adversities of many people. They have failed to heed His instruction to keep away from idols. The verse says, *"I said to you, 'I am the Lord your God; do not worship the gods of the Amorites, in whose land you live.' But you have not listened to me."* (Judges 6:10)

As I waited further on the Lord, He began to show me some of the foreign gods of the land of America which many believers are worshipping. These are the things I wrote down:

- Fame & Popularity
- Power & Control
- Money & Fortune
- Luxury
- Sex
- Worldly Comfort
- Independence
- Human philosophies
- Titles and appellations
- Appearance

Is there any of these idols erected in the temple of your life? Is there any of these that competes with your allegiance to the King? Then you must get rid of it before you can truly restore the altar in your life. In the passage we just cited, Gideon had to pull down the altar of baal before he could raise an altar to the Lord for freedom to be restored to the nation of Israel which was under Midianite oppression.

Every altar in your life which is not raised to the Lord must be pulled down and destroyed. If Manasseh could succeed to destroy his idols and the evil altars he had built in the Lord's temple then you too, with the help of the Holy Spirit, can dismantle and discard every such altar in your life.

When Elijah was to restore worship in the nation of Israel after Ahab and Jezebel had instituted baal worship in the land, he started by repairing the Lord's altar which was in ruins. The Bible says, *"Then Elijah said to all the people, 'Come here to me.' They came to him, and he repaired the altar of the Lord, which had been torn down."* (1Kings 18:30)

For there to be any meaningful restoration in your own life, you have to restore the temple and the altar. Repair the altar of prayer, praise, worship, thanksgiving and sacrifice in your life. Let your altars speak for you against every evil altar raised against you. The Lord will help you make the necessary repairs if you are willing.

Restoration of Worship

The Lord promised that in the days of restoration he is going to restore David's fallen tent. If you read the scriptures, you will realize that the tent David built to house the Ark of the Covenant was a place of incessant, unadulterated, and continuous worship to the Lord Almighty. Remember the Lord Jesus said,

"²³ Yet a time is coming and has now come when the true worshipers will worship the Father in the Spirit and in truth, for they are the kind of worshipers the Father seeks. ²⁴ God is spirit, and his worshipers must worship in the Spirit and in truth." (John 4:23).

This is the time to worship the Father in Spirit and in truth. And the way the Father is raising such worshippers is by rebuilding and restoring the fallen tent of David, where hands will be constantly lifted up to God.

He has promised that, He *"will return and rebuild David's fallen tent. Its ruins I will rebuild, and I will restore it"* (Acts 15: 16). Beloved we are in that time of restoration of true worship to the Holy God of heaven.

Get ready to be endowed with a heavenly capacity to worship God with an intensity you never knew before. Get ready to be thrust into the Holy of holies and prostrate yourself before the Majestic One seated on His Holy Throne. If you have never known true worship or lost the ability to worship the Lord, now is the time to say, *"Lord, teach me to worship, help me worship you like I never did."*

Restoration to Service

Many people serving are in the service of man, organizations, systems, denominations, ministries etc. instead of being in the service of the Lord. Some are serving themselves under religious banners in the name of serving the Lord. For many, they are the origin of the towers and castles of religious formalities in the name of Christian service.

Some who started well have been derailed into self-service because of the pursuit of gain and fame. In the name of religious tolerance some have abandoned the truth to preach and teach what the masses want to hear. Their message is carefully designed to increase their ratings in the worldly system at the detriment of the souls of men who need to hear the unadulterated truth of God's holy word.

It was in such a situation that the prophet Jeremiah found himself. He compromised the word of God in order to say what the people wanted to hear and so, though he still appeared as the prophet of the Lord, to God he was no longer in His service. That is why the Lord said to him,

> *"Therefore this is what the Lord says: 'If you repent, I will restore you that you may serve me; if you utter worthy, not worthless, words, you will be my spokesman. Let this people turn to you, but you must not turn to them.'"*

(Jeremiah 15:19)

Maybe you have been serving a system, denomination, organization, yourself or any other thing thinking you were serving the Lord. God says for you to be restored to His service you have to repent and abandon your compromise with the philosophies of this world, and creeds of religious systems and begin to speak the word of God and only the word of God. He wants to make you His spokesperson to this generation.

May we never be deceived by our own schemes under the disguise of the service of the Lord! God cannot be deceived; many people need to face the truth that their service may not be a service unto the Lord. They may be serving for their own financial or material security. They may be serving for the recognition and applause of men. They may be serving for fame and popularity in the world, but they are not serving the Lord.

May be you have recognized that you have been serving a system or yourself rather than serving the Lord. You can ask the Lord to restore you to His service and make you a spokesperson of His. Restoration to God's service is part of the promise of restoration for you.

In this chapter we have concentrated on that which is of paramount importance to you, that is, your relationship with God and your service to God. These are the most important aspects of restoration because they have eternal consequences. In the next chapter we are going to look at aspects of restoration that have to do with external things, namely what you have.

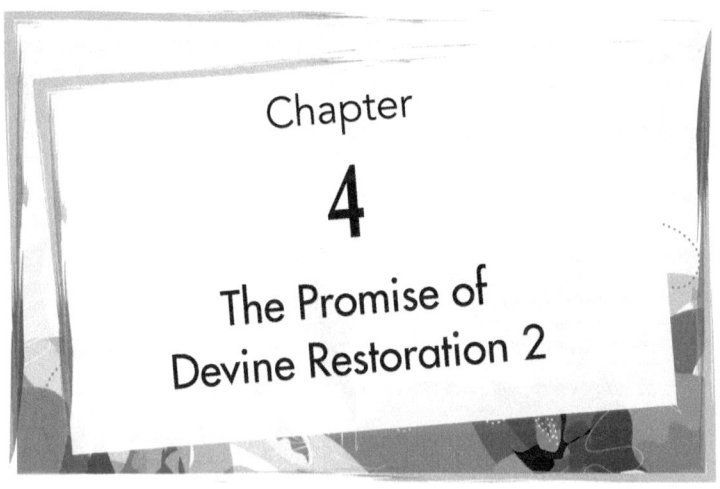

Chapter 4

The Promise of Devine Restoration 2

Restoration of Fortunes

Many of us have lost our fortunes to one adversity or another. Worse still many are there who have never been able to get the fortunes that are rightfully theirs as heirs of the riches that Christ died to bring to suffering mankind.

The Lord has promise to restore your fortunes. The pages of the Book are littered with promises of the restoration of fortunes. It means even what you were ordained to have but which you have never been able to lay hands on because of the circumstances of life will be restored to you.

We are a in a season of restoration of fortunes, those who believe and go for it will experience it. Here are some of the promises of restoration of fortunes:

> *"This is what the Lord says: '"18 I will restore the fortunes of Jacob's tents and have compassion on his dwellings; the city will be rebuilt on her ruins, and the palace will stand in its proper place. 19 From them will come songs of thanksgiving and the sound of rejoicing. I will add to their numbers, and they will not be decreased; I will bring them honor, and they will not be disdained."*
>
> (Jeremiah 30: 18-19)

> *10 "This is what the Lord says: 'You say about this place, "It is a desolate waste, without people or animals." Yet in the towns of Judah and the streets of Jerusalem that are deserted, inhabited by neither people nor animals, there will be heard once more 11 the sounds of joy and gladness, the voices of bride and bridegroom, and the voices of those who bring thank offerings to the house of the Lord, saying, "Give thanks to the Lord Almighty, for the Lord is good; his love endures forever." For I will restore the fortunes of the land as they were before, ' says the Lord."*
>
> (Jeremiah 33:10-11)

> *"Therefore this is what the Sovereign LORD says: I will now restore the fortunes of Jacob and will have compassion on all the people of Israel, and I will be zealous for my holy name."*
> (Ezekiel 39:25)

The Lord has promised to restore your fortunes, for you are of the house of Jacob. Everything in your life that is in ruins will be rebuilt and restored to you. Along with the restoration of your fortunes will come gladness, rejoicing, thank offerings, and celebrations.

There will be increase in your life because of the restoration of your fortunes. Increase is coming to you. Honor and dignity will be restored to your life because of the fortunes that restoration is bringing to you. You have been mocked despised and disdained enough.

This is the season for your elevation. You have mourned and wept enough, this is the season for you celebration. When fortunes are restored, then will we hear frequently the voice of bride and bridegroom. It is the season of restoration for you, go for full and total restoration. You have been afflicted enough, now is the time to laugh and dance. Now is the time to walk with your head lifted high. Like Job, it is the season for you to receive double of everything that the storms of life deprived you of.

Restoration of Inheritances

One of the things which are very evident in the New Testament Church is that we have failed to live up to that which is our inheritance in the Lord. We have failed to appropriate the benefits of the completed and accomplished work of Calvary for ourselves and loved ones. It seems as though many, because of indulgence and sinful compromise like Esau, have forfeited the very inheritances that were meant to be theirs because of the allegiance to the King of the universes.

Whatever it is you have lost because of foolishness, and whatever it is you have not been able to experience because of ignorance, the Lord is going to restore to you. Get ready to experience the things you have not experienced, get ready to step into new territories of your inheritance in the Lord.

When David got to the throne of Israel, after a while he remembered his covenant with Jonathan and asked if there was any member of the family of Saul who was still alive so he could show him favor because of Jonathan. When they searched, they found a son of Jonathan called Mephibosheth who was living in misery and poverty. In fact the name of the town he lived in was called Lodebar which when translated means without pasture. He was the grandson of a former king but was living in poverty. He had forfeited his inheritance because of the wickedness of his grandfather.

And how many are there who are not able to enter their inheritance or become what was ordained for them because of the sins of their fathers! You have authority to break every limitation that has been placed on you because of the lineage you came from. I treated this topic in details in my book ***"Making a Difference: How to Effect Lasting Change."***

When Mephibosheth was brought before David, this is what David said to him,

> *"⁷ Don't be afraid," David said to him, "for I will surely show you kindness for the sake of your father Jonathan. I will restore to you all the land that belonged to your grandfather Saul, and you will always eat at my table. "*
> *⁸ Mephibosheth bowed down and said, "What is your servant, that you should notice a dead dog like me?"*
> *⁹ Then the king summoned Ziba, Saul's steward, and said to him, "I have given your master's grandson everything that belonged to Saul and his family. ¹⁰ You and your sons and your servants are to farm the land for him and bring in the crops, so that your master's grandson may be provided for. And Mephibosheth, grandson of your master, will*

> *always eat at my table." (Now Ziba had fifteen sons and twenty servants.)*
> *11 Then Ziba said to the king, "Your servant will do whatever my lord the king commands his servant to do." So Mephibosheth ate at David's[a] table like one of the king's sons.*
> *12 Mephibosheth had a young son named Mika, and all the members of Ziba's household were servants of Mephibosheth. 13 And Mephibosheth lived in Jerusalem, because he always ate at the king's table; he was lame in both feet."*

(2 Samuel 9:7-13)

Like Mephibosheth you may be living without pasture in your Lodebar. The Bible says, *"He makes me to lie down in green pastures"* so why are you living without pastures when green pastures should be your inheritance?

Why are you living in hiding when you were meant to be in the limelight? Just like the covenant between David and Jonathan constrained David to fetch the son of Jonathan from his hiding in the land of no pasture, we have a stronger covenant with the King of the universe, sealed by His own very blood. I see you being fetched from your Lodebar to your Jerusalem. I see you being restored to eat from the table of the King.

David said the Lord prepares a table before him, so it's your inheritance to feed from the Kings table. You have eaten crumbs for too long. It is your season to eat from the table. Mephibosheth was living in Lodebar with Makir which means *"sold"*. In other words he had been sold to lack and poverty. Whatever sold you to lack and poverty, the King has redeemed you.

He says in His word that *"You were sold for nothing, and without money you will be redeemed."* (Isaiah 52:3) The price for your redemption from lack, want, and poverty was paid by the death of the Lamb of God. Nothing has the right to keep you in poverty any longer. The King wants to restore your heavenly Father's estate to you.

I see you possessing your possessions. The cattle and wealth on a thousand hills are His and therefore by right of inheritance yours. I see men given to serve you and work for you. Everyone who has cheated you of anything that was rightfully yours will bring it back trembling.

It is your season of restoration. It is time to feed on the abundance in the courts of the King. It is time for people to work and bring the proceeds to you. It's the season of restoration of inheritances.

> *8 This is what the Lord says: "In the time of my favor I will answer you, and in the day of salvation I will help you; I*

> *will keep you and will make you to be a covenant for the people, to restore the land and to reassign its desolate inheritances, ⁹ to say to the captives, 'Come out,' and to those in darkness, 'Be free!' They will feed beside the roads and find pasture on every barren hill. ¹⁰ They will neither hunger nor thirst, nor will the desert heat or the sun beat down on them. He who has compassion on them will guide them and lead them beside springs of water. ¹¹ I will turn all my mountains into roads, and my highways will be raised up."*
>
> (Isaiah 49:8-11)

The Lord Jesus is the fulfillment of that prophecy. He has come to reassign to us our lost inheritance. He has come to restore to us our land and to cause us to find pasture of on every barren hill. No more hunger, no more thirst. It is time for you to be led beside springs of water and to travel on highways.

We are in the season of reassignment of inheritances. That which your fathers were not able to possess is within your reach. It says no longer will the desert heat or the sun beat down on you. This means you will move from an air conditioned home to an air conditioned car to an air conditioned office. You have walked under the sun for too long. You should be tired of the heat. It is time to enter your inheritance.

Restoration of Boundaries

There is a king in the Bible about whom it is said, *"He was the one who restored the boundaries of Israel from Lebo Hamath to the Dead Sea, in accordance with the word of the Lord, the God of Israel, spoken through his servant Jonah son of Amittai, the prophet from Gath Hepher."* (2 Kings 14:25)

Like Israel of old many of us are living in narrowed down boundaries. Our enemies seem to have pushed us back and narrowed the scope of our influence. Worse still, many are they who have not yet explored the limits of their inheritance for fear of the enemy that must be driven out. It is time to restore our boundaries!

I read a promise somewhere in the Book that says, *"The day for building your walls will come, the day for extending your boundaries."* (Micah 7:11) I believe we are in that day, the day of restoring and extending our boundaries. We are in the season of Jabez, the season of extension of our borders. It is time to cry out to the Lord, *"Oh, that you would bless me and enlarge my territory! Let your hand be with me, and keep me from harm so that I will be free from pain."* (1Chronicles 4:10)

Let us ask for the extension of our spiritual, social, intellectual, financial, material, and physical borders. We are destined for far more territories than we have experienced or possessed. I hear the Lord saying to the church *"²Enlarge the place of your tent, stretch your tent curtains wide, do not hold back; lengthen your cords, strengthen your stakes. ³For you will spread out to the right and to the left; your descendants will dispossess nations and settle in their desolate cities."* (Isaiah 54:2-3)

This is the season of enlargement, stretching, and spreading in all directions. The Lord says, *"Do not hold back"*. It means you are the only person who can keep yourself from expanding and extending your boundaries. I do not want to remain in this limited place I am in spiritually, financially, materially, socially, intellectually, professionally, and otherwise. I don't know about you but like Jabez I am going in for total and unprecedented expansion and extension. If you decide that you are responding to the call of the Lord for expansion, then your boundaries will truly be extended beyond your wildest imagination.

No enemy will be able to stop you. If they could not stop Jabez, then they will not be able to stop you. If God could answer the prayer of Jabez, then He will answer yours. For you are in a better covenant than Jabez was! It's time to restore our boundaries so that like David you can say, *"⁵Lord, you alone are my portion and my cup; you make my lot secure. ⁶The boundary lines have fallen for me in pleasant places; surely I have a delightful inheritance"* (Psalm 16:5-6).

Restoration of walls

> *"Your people will rebuild the ancient ruins and will raise up the age-old foundations; you will be called Repairer of Broken Walls, Restorer of Streets with Dwellings."*
>
> (Isaiah 58:12)

The Lord has given you the ability to rebuild ruins and turn them into habitable dwellings. The ills in society today are due to ruined lives, ruined homes, broken foundations, and broken walls. The enemy has easy access into lives because the walls of defense are all broken and therefore he is free to move in and out of lives and homes at random. Let us rebuild the walls of respect, compassion, mercy, peace, and grace. Let us rebuild the foundations of love, truth, transparency, and integrity. Let us rebuild the walls of honesty, self-control, and contentment. If the walls are rebuilt, lives will be restored. Homes will be restored and society will be restored. It is because these walls are broken both in the church and in society that the enemy has free reign to attack and influence.

The Bible says, *"Like a city whose walls are broken through is a person who lacks self-control."* (Proverbs 25:28) a City without walls is a defenseless and vulnerable city. In those days, a city was only as strong and defensive as its walls. So if we lack self-control in our lives, homes, churches, and society in general then we become like cities without walls, and therefore a playground for the enemy. As we rebuild the walls then our lives and homes will be restored.

Chapter 5

The Promise of Divine Restoration 3

Restoration of Health

> *"But I will restore you to health and heal your wounds,' declares the Lord, 'because you are called an outcast, Zion for whom no one cares.'"*
>
> (Jeremiah 30:17)

I don't know which area of your life or personality is suffering from a wound. It doesn't matter where you have been wounded. The Lord has promised restoration to health for you. Many people are wounded mentally, emotionally, and even spiritually. You see many people outwardly whole but inwardly broken and in need of healing. God wants to bind the wounds inflicted on you by people or life's circumstances. Not only does He want to heal your wounds, He also wants to heal your diseases, sicknesses, and infirmities. The Lord Jesus paid the price for your healing. The Lord says he doesn't just want to heal you but to restore you to health.

The Lord is the God who restores from the sickbed to perfect health and wholeness. Somewhere in the Book it is written that

> *"The Lord sustains them on their sickbed and restores them from their bed of illness."*
>
> (Psalm 41:3)

and

> *"...then that person can pray to God and find favor with him, they will see God's face and shout for joy; he will restore them to full well-being."*
>
> (Job 33:26)

The Lord is interested in restoring you to full well-being, body, soul, and spirit; every part of your being made whole. This is the season to be free from every disease, sickness, infirmity or affliction that has plagued you until now. It is time to rise from the sickbed and be made whole again. It is the season of restoration to emotional, mental, physical, and social wholeness. Yeah, it is time to be restored to full well-being, nothing less should be accepted or settled for.

Restoration of Joy

True Holy Ghost inspired or generated joy is lacking in many lives or Christian gatherings. We have tried had to produced our own joy and have failed woefully. God wants to restore His joy in your life and in the Church. This means everything that has deprived you of the joy of the Lord will be far removed from you.

Sinful compromise is one of the many things that deprive many of the joy of the Lord. Many have lost the pure joy of salvation and are in pursuit of joy from things and places that can offer no true or lasting joy.

David experienced the horror of losing the joy of salvation when he sinned with Bathsheba and murdered her husband. After the prophet of God confronted him with his sin, he repented and asked the Lord to restore to him the joy of salvation. David prayed, *"Restore to me the joy of your salvation and grant me a willing spirit, to sustain me"* (Psalm 51:12) If you have lost the joy of the Lord, the joy of salvation, you don't need to try to be joyful on your own or seek joy from sources which can offer no joy. Seek the joy of the Lord by asking Him to restore to you His joy.

Also as you receive the restoration of the other aspects of the promise of restoration, the joy of the Lord will fill your soul, as you will find new reason to celebrate. Now is the time to celebrate. You have been mournful and sorrowful for too long. Now is the time to put on the garment of joy and rejoice in the Lord your God. It is time to be radiant and exude with joy and gladness. Because it is time of restoration it is also the time of rejoicing and gladness that has a heavenly origin. *"... When God restores his people, let Jacob rejoice and Israel be glad!"* (Psalm 53:6)

Restoration of Comfort

Some of the immediate effects of restoration to health are comfort and peace. Nothing causes pain and discomfort like wounds, sickness, and diseases. Also, when there is joy, there is comfort and because there is restoration of joy, there is restoration of comfort. The Lord says,

> *18 I have seen their ways, but I will heal them; I will guide them and restore comfort to Israel's mourners, 19 creating praise on their lips. Peace, peace, to those far and near," says the Lord. "And I will heal them."*
>
> (Isaiah 57:18-19)

You have mourned enough, you have been in pain enough, it is time to be comforted. Healing, peace, and comfort come in the same package as we see in the above verses. You can't have one without the other. As you enter your restoration to health, the peace and comfort of the Lord will fill you.

Restoration of Dominion

When God created mankind, he endowed us with ability to exercise dominion over the rest of terrestrial creation. He gave us the ability to rule and subdue the earth but because of the fall we lost all that ability. Now, then Christ Jesus came as a man to regain and restore to fellow man the lost dominion. However many of us are yet to enter the realm of dominion. We live in fear instead of exercising dominion. We are ruled by circumstances instead of ruling. The elements dictate to us what we should do and when instead of us controlling and dominating the elements.

In this season of restoration, the past dominion that mankind had in the Garden of Eden will be restored to us. It is the season to exercise dominion like you never did before. In the job market and business, over sicknesses and diseases, over witches and demons, over nature and circumstances, dominion must be exercised. This is His promise to you,

> "As for you, watchtower of the flock, stronghold of Daughter Zion, the former dominion will be restored to you; kingship will come to Daughter of Jerusalem."
>
> (Micah 4:8)

It is your season to reign and dominate and rule the things around you. This is the season to punish the works and workers of darkness. It is our season to live like the kings we have been made to be by the death of the King on the cross.

Restoration of Splendor

Because it is time for restoration of dominion and kingship, it is also the time for restoration of splendor, for kings exercise dominion in splendor. It is your time to shine in kingly splendor. Let men and women be attracted to the splendor you are about to be clothed in, and seek the God of your splendor.

Those who have despised you will look at you with awe and respect because of the restoration of splendor that is coming upon you. The world will be amazed at the splendor that is coming upon the church. We shall not go unnoticed any longer.

Just like Adam was clothed in splendor in the Garden of Eden, the Lord wants to restore that same splendor to you. He says,

> *"The Lord will restore the splendor of Jacob like the splendor of Israel, though destroyers have laid them waste and have ruined their vines."*
>
> (Nahum 2:2)

Yes! That is the restoration of prevailing splendor, receive it!

Restoration of Harvest

Many people plant but are not able to reap because one thing or another destroys their harvest. They work hard but cannot enjoy the fruit of their labor. They invest but cannot reap the proceeds of their investment. Many are like the Israelites in Judges Chapter 6 who always planted but had their crops constantly destroyed by the Midianites and Amalekites just before the crops could reach maturity.

The Lord said when He restores your fortunes it will come with an abundant harvest. So during this season of restoration, every seed you ever sowed which did not bring you the expected harvest will germinate and bring you an abundant harvest. It is time you call forth dormant seeds in the ground of time to grow, blossom, and bring forth fruits. Every barren area of your life will be made healthy and bring forth abundant fruits.

Surely he has done great things!

^{21} Do not be afraid, land of Judah; be glad and rejoice. Surely the Lord has done great things! ^{22} Do not be afraid, you wild animals, for the pastures in the wilderness are becoming green. The trees are bearing their fruit; the fig tree and the vine yield their riches. ^{23} Be glad, people of Zion, rejoice in the Lord your God, for he has given you the autumn rains because he is faithful. He sends you abundant showers, both autumn and spring rains, as before. ^{24} The threshing floors will be filled with grain; the vats will overflow with new wine and oil. ^{25} "I will repay you for the years the locusts have eaten — the great locust and the young locust, the other locusts and the locust swarm—my great army that I sent among you. ^{26} You will have plenty to eat, until you are full, and you will praise the name of the Lord your God, who has worked wonders for you; never again will my people be shamed. ^{27} Then you will know that I am in Israel, that I am the Lord your God, and that there is no other; never again will my people be shamed."

(Joel 2:21-27)

God is restoring your harvest, both physical and spiritual!

Chapter 6

The Promise of Divine Restoration 4

Restoration of Leaders

One of the greatest needs be it in the home, the church, or society at large is that of leaders in the true sense of the word. The world is crying for leaders. Individuals are crying for true and authentic leadership. Many people in leadership positions today do not qualify to be leaders, because they serve themselves and their interest instead of serving the people and God's interest.

The world needs leaders who will lay down their lives for the ones they are leading. Leaders who will sacrifice their comfort and gain for the welfare of those they are called to lead. The world needs leaders with no secret agenda, interests, or motives, but the welfare and wellbeing of their followers. Many a home is broken because true leadership is lacking. Society is broken because the leaders of today are out to fatten themselves from the labors of the people.

We need Moseses, Samuels, Nehemiahs, Davids and many others like them in this generation. The cry of the Father is to raise leaders, true shepherds in every sphere of society who will bleed for the people, leaders who will refuse to eat until the people have eaten and are satisfied, leaders who feel the pain of the people, and are hurt when the people are hurting. That is why the Lord has promised, *"I will restore your leaders as in days of old, your rulers as at the beginning. Afterward you will be called the City of Righteousness, the Faithful City."* (Isaiah 1:26)

God says when the leaders are restored as of old, afterwards the city will be called the city of righteousness, the faithful city. This tells us that, a home, church, city, or nation is a reflection of the leadership. May be you are desperate to see true leadership restored. It is time to hold on to the Lord to restore our leaders. True leadership will be restored to homes, churches, and society at large. It is the season of restoration of leaders as of old.

Restoration of Vision

One of the roles of true leadership is to provide vision and direction. And where there is no vision there is no restrain. That is the reason for the chaos we find everywhere in the church today and in society at large. People seem to have cast off every restrain because of lack of vision.

The Lord Jesus restored the vision of several people in the New Testament. Though theirs were physical sight, I believe the Lord is in the business of restoring vision to individuals, homes, churches, and society at large. It is time to receive a restoration of your vision.

Like Saul in the book of Acts, scales will fall off from your eyes so you can see God's plan and direction for your life. Heaven is in the business of releasing dreams and vision into willing hearts and minds. It is time to receive vision from above. You need not spend one more day without an outcry for a vision from above until you have received it.

Restoration of Families

There are many parents with broken and aching hearts bleeding for their children who have run away from home. Mothers are weeping for their sons and daughters wondering if they will ever return home, if they do, will they return whole? Families are broken, homes and lives shattered, but in these days of restoration, God is in the business of restoring family life to many.

These are the days of Elijah, the days of restoration of families. Once again fathers will feel for their sons and sons for their fathers. The hostility that the enemy has planted between fathers and sons will be taken away. It is the season of restoration.

The Lord says, *"⁵ See, I will send the prophet Elijah to you before that great and dreadful day of the Lord comes. ⁶ He will turn the hearts of the parents to their children, and the hearts of the children to their parents…"* (Malachi 4:5-6). It is time for harmony to be restored in homes where hostility has reigned. And for those parents who are yearning for the return of runaway children in captivity to drugs and other delinquent behaviors, there is a promise of restoration for them too.

The Lord says,

> *This is what the Sovereign Lord says: "See, I will beckon to the nations, I will lift up my banner to the peoples; they will bring your sons in their arms and carry your daughters on their hips."*

(Isaiah 49:22)

> *⁴ "Lift up your eyes and look about you: All assemble and come to you; your sons come from afar, and your daughters are carried on the hip. ⁵ Then you will look and be radiant, your heart will throb and swell with joy; the wealth on the seas will be brought to you, to you the riches of the nations will come."*
>
> (Isaiah 60: 4-5)

You can begin to celebrate because your children are coming back home. It is the season of restoration of families. Joy and radiance is coming back to your countenance because your children are coming back home. The Lord is going to wipe the tears of your longing and replace them with tears of joyous celebration. And behold, they are not coming back empty-handed!

Now that we have seen the scope of restoration, the pathway to restoration, and the different aspects or facets of the promise of restoration, I want us to look at some specific biblical examples of divine restoration. This way we will better understand God's promise to bring about restoration in the lives of His chosen ones. As we look at these lives, you are going to see each chapter of this study coming to play in the restoration process.

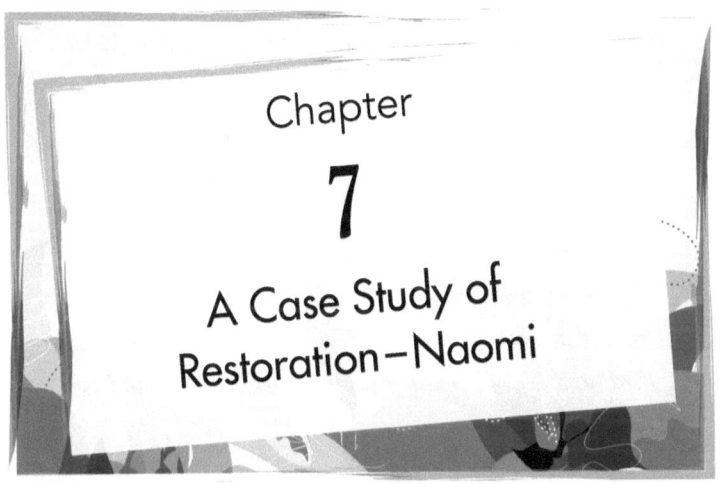

Chapter 7

A Case Study of Restoration – Naomi

Naomi's story is a candid example of the promise of divine restoration. This story narrated in the pages of the book of Ruth in the Old Testament shows that no situation is beyond the redeeming and restoring power of the LORD God of Hosts. The Lord wants to bring a complete, full, and total restoration in your life even as He did for Naomi.

When Life is a Contradiction

"¹ In the days when the judges ruled, there was a famine in the land. So a man from Bethlehem in Judah, together with his wife and two sons, went to live for a while in

> the country of Moab. ² The man's name was Elimelek, his wife's name was Naomi, and the names of his two sons were Mahlon and Kilion. They were Ephrathites from Bethlehem, Judah. And they went to Moab and lived there. ³ Now Elimelek, Naomi's husband, died, and she was left with her two sons. ⁴ They married Moabite women, one named Orpah and the other Ruth. After they had lived there about ten years, ⁵ both Mahlon and Kilion also died, and Naomi was left without her two sons and her husband."
>
> (Ruth 1:1-5)

If we look carefully at the names of the characters in the passage and the things which befell them, then we see that sometimes life is a contradiction. Let us explain some of the contradictions that crowded the life of this family in study.

- Elimelek means *"my God is King"*
- Naomi means *"my pleasantness"*
- Mahlon means *"sick"*
- Kilion means *"pining"*
- Ephrata means *"fruitfulness"*
- Bethlehem means *"house of bread"*

The very first contradiction we see in this story is that there was a famine in the land of fruitfulness. Ephrata which means fruitfulness couldn't produce fruits for crops that were planted there and the result was a severe famine. Fruitful had become barren, lack had crept in where abundance should reign; there was famine in the fruitful land.

The second contradiction which is a direct result of the first is that Bethlehem, the house of bread had no bread. People living in the house of bread had no food to eat. There was serious hunger and lack in the house of bread. What a contradiction. Indeed sometimes life is full of contradictions.

The third contradiction is that Elimelek and Naomi named the blessings of God according to their circumstances. The Bible says children are a gift from God. As Jews, this couple understood the importance of names but they decided to name their blessings with curse words.

When God gave them the first blessings, they named it *"sick"*. May be they were looking at their circumstance of famine. May be the child was born sick or with some deformity and they decided to name the child according to what they were experiencing instead of according to what they believed God would do.

The second blessing from God was named *"pining"*. Again may be the famine was causing them to pine away, may be the child was born with a disease or syndrome that caused him to pine away.

I believe Elimelek and Naomi were just reacting according to their circumstances. They chose to identify their blessings with the harshness of their circumstances instead of with the goodness of their God. What a contradiction, that *"my God is king"* and *"my pleasantness"* will give birth to *"sick"* and *"pining"*.

What Naomi and Elimelek did here is that they cursed the blessings of God by choosing to name their blessings according to circumstantial evidence of the adversity in which they found themselves. And the sad truth is that there are many people who despise the blessings of God just like this couple did. They concentrate too much on their circumstances that they fail to glorify God in their words, actions, and all else they do. They refuse to be grateful for the blessings God has given them in the midst of their adversity.

The fourth contradiction is that unpleasantness came into the life of one named *"pleasantness"*. Naomi lost her husband, and two sons. These are not pleasant things, not things that should happen to anyone. So the things that were happening in her life were things that contradicted her name.

Do not Act in Error

Because of the pressure and contradiction in which Elimelek and Naomi found themselves, they made several errors.

First, they identified themselves with the famine by naming the blessings of God with negativity. The lesson here for you is you should never identify yourself with your negative circumstances. Do not speak the language of your circumstances. Always learn to appreciate the Lord for His blessings to you, however they come. Never fail to acknowledge the goodness and favor of God upon your life even in the midst of contradictory circumstances.

The second error they made was that they moved away on their own initiative to go settle in Moab. They acted according to the pressures of their circumstances instead of according to divine instructions. Though they physically separated from the famine, because they had identified themselves with a famine situation by the names they gave their children, the famine followed them into Moab. They carried along the famine identity into Moab and suffered for it. Lesson here for you is never move until Jehovah asks you to.

The third error Naomi made was to lose faith in God. Remember, Elimelek, *"my God is King"* had died. In order words

Naomi had lost faith in the sovereignty and kingship of the Lord God Jehovah even over famine, loss, and contradictions. She thought God was no longer in control of the situation, and so *"my God is King"* died. To Naomi her God was now dead because he had *"failed to act"* when Naomi expected Him to. My dear friend, never lose your faith in the sovereignty of God. Never fail to acknowledge that Jehovah is in control and rules over circumstances.

The fourth error she made was to disobey the word of God to the Jewish people, namely that they should not intermarry with the surrounding nations. Never compromise the word of God in the midst of contradictory circumstances. The reason Naomi allowed her sons to marry Moabite women is because she had lost faith in God.

When a man or woman loses faith in the Sovereignty of Jehovah, then they begin to act according to the impulse of the moment. The word of God becomes conditional and can be negotiated when one no longer believes that God is in absolute control. Lesson here for you is that never negotiate the word of God.

Because Naomi acted in error she
- Lost her faith in God as King (see verses 13 & 20)
- She lost her life of praise and worship (verse 3)

- She lost the blessings she wasn't grateful for (verse 5)
- She became bitter and empty (verses 20 to 21)

The Secret to Restoration

*"⁶When Naomi heard in Moab that the Lord had come to the aid of his people by providing food for them, she and her daughters-in-law prepared to return home from there. ⁷With her two daughters-in-law she left the place where she had been living and **set out on the road that would take them back to the land of Judah.**"*

(Ruth 1:6-7, emphasis added)

That is the secret right there in bold. When they heard that God had come to the aid of His people they took a decision to return to the land of praise, the land of fruitfulness, and the house of bread. They could have heard and not acted. They could have heard and stayed where they were, but they took the decision to set out on the road that would lead them to the place of restoration.

Just like I have shared with you the many benefits that are yours in this season of restoration and showed you the path to restoration, the determinant factor is your decision to set out on that path to restoration until you receive your full and complete restoration.

The Bible says, *"So the two women went on until they came to Bethlehem."* (Ruth 1:19) the phrase *"went until…"* tells us that it was not child's play. The road back to restoration is not an easy way. It is not short, easy, or smooth. It requires effort and persistence to total restoration, but it pays off big.

Persistent determination is the key to breakthrough. Life is looking for people with persistence and determination to grant them access to new heights and new dimensions. Every obstacle bows to persistent determination. It is the passport through the gates of accomplishment and establishment. It is the line that separates winners from losers, victors from victims. God rewards persistent determination. The secret to success is to *"continue until…"* You must refuse to stop until you have reached your Bethlehem.

Lessons on Relationships

> *⁸ Then Naomi said to her two daughters-in-law, "Go back, each of you, to your mother's home. May the Lord show you kindness, as you have shown kindness to your dead husbands and to me. ⁹ May the Lord grant that each of you will find rest in the home of another husband."*
>
> *Then she kissed them goodbye and they wept aloud 10 and said to her, "We will go back with you to your people."*

11 But Naomi said, "Return home, my daughters. Why would you come with me? Am I going to have any more sons, who could become your husbands? 12 Return home, my daughters; I am too old to have another husband. Even if I thought there was still hope for me—even if I had a husband tonight and then gave birth to sons— 13 would you wait until they grew up? Would you remain unmarried for them? No, my daughters. It is more bitter for me than for you, because the Lord's hand has turned against me!" 14 At this they wept aloud again. Then Orpah kissed her mother-in-law goodbye, but Ruth clung to her. 15 "Look," said Naomi, "your sister-in-law is going back to her people and her gods. Go back with her." 16 But Ruth replied, "Don't urge me to leave you or to turn back from you. Where you go I will go, and where you stay I will stay. Your people will be my people and your God my God. 17 Where you die I will die, and there I will be buried. May the Lord deal with me, be it ever so severely, if even death separates you and me." 18 When Naomi realized that Ruth was determined to go with her, she stopped urging her. 19 So the two women went on until they came to Bethlehem. When they arrived in Bethlehem, the whole town was stirred because of them, and the women exclaimed, "Can this be Naomi?"

(Ruth 1:8-19)

There are several lessons on relationships I want us to look at before we continue our study on restoration. This is very important because it will greatly determine how far we embrace divine restoration.

The first lesson on relationships I want you to take home from this study of Naomi is that not everyone who is part of your pain will stick with you in life. Orpah was part of the pain Naomi felt but she didn't stick with Naomi. If you understand this, then you will always give others the freedom of choice, to grow with you, or to grow without you. You must make room for others to grow and become better no matter how indebted they are to you.

Naomi gave both Ruth and Orpah the opportunity to better their lives apart from hers. She gave them room for expansion. Like Naomi, learn to bless those who want to leave and release them to go wherever they think growth and expansion can be found. When you bind people to yourself, you limit them and therefore limit yourself because people who are not meant to be in your life will keep out those who were meant to be.

Second lesson you must take home is that, God will bring into your life both Orpahs and Ruths. The Orpahs will one day leave for greener pastures, for a better life without you.

A Case Study of Restoration – Naomi

This does not make them bad or indifferent to your situation. It simply means they were meant for a season or came for a reason. Keeping or holding on to Orpahs will frustrate both you and them.

You must understand that everything you release or give up, which was meant to be yours will always return to you later with an increase. Anything you release and it goes without coming back to you was not meant to be yours, it was meant for some other person. When it leaves, it makes room for what it yours to come to you. The reason many people do not receive what is theirs is because they hold on to what is somebody else's.

The third lesson I want to bring to your attention is that there is always someone who will stick with you through thick and thin, high and low, better or worse, someone on divine assignment. These are the Ruths who through personal commitment and divine arrangement will stay with you for a lifetime. They will often be committed to you beyond logical reasoning. They may even give up personal opportunities for growth to ensure your well-being.

Ruths come with a heart bonding beyond anything the eyes can explain. Their commitment is independent of what others say of, think of, or do to you. They establish a heart bonding which nothing from outside can break. If anything, external circumstances only strengthen the bonds.

Ruths insist on staying even when asked to go, they follow wherever God leads you, they are not attracted by the beauty or comfort of where you live neither are they deterred by the ugliness or discomfort of where you live.

Ruths embrace your existing and new relationships, they accept those who are part of your life and become part of your entourage. Ruths embrace your spirituality and support your commitment to your God. However, you cannot expect everybody to be a Ruth to you. In life you must understand the blessing of having Orpahs too and celebrate their presence in your life as long as they are there, and celebrate their departure when it is time for them to leave.

The God Who Restores

> *"13 So Boaz took Ruth and she became his wife. When he made love to her, **the Lord enabled her to conceive, and she gave birth to a son.** 14 The women said to Naomi: **"Praise be to the Lord, who this day has not left you without a guardian-redeemer. May he become famous throughout Israel! 15 He will renew your life and sustain you in your old age. For your daughter-in-law, who***

A Case Study of Restoration – Naomi

> *loves you and who is better to you than seven sons, has given him birth."*
> *16 Then Naomi took the child in her arms and cared for him. 17 The women living there said, "**Naomi has a son!**" And they named him Obed. He was the father of Jesse, the father of David."*
>
> (Ruth 4:13-17, emphasis added)

In spite of the fact that Naomi had lost everything, once she set herself on the path to restoration, nothing could stop her from entering into full restoration. In this story there was not only restoration for Naomi but also for Ruth. Ruth who had lost her husband and had no child received a double restoration of a husband and a child. Because this study is on the life of Naomi I want us to concentrate on Naomi.

The Bible says the Lord enables Ruth to conceive. It means Ruth was barren and therefore needed divine intervention in order to become a mother. And God did it so that Naomi could have a son. I do not know what area of your life is in need of divine intervention for there to be restoration.

If God could enable Ruth to conceive a baby so as to bring restoration in the life of Naomi, there is nothing that would be impossible for you with divine enabling. God will enable you conceive ideas, dreams, and visions that will lead to restoration. God can use the Ruths in your life to bring you restoration. Divine enabling will come when you walk in divine principles.

God is a God of restoration, even in Naomi's anger, disappointment, emptiness, and bitterness towards God, once she embarked on that road to restoration, God overrode all that and blessed her beyond her wildest expectations.

There is nothing that can stop God's plan and purposes for a generation. The devil's intent was to wipe out the lineage of Naomi to prevent the lineage of the Messiah from taking root. He killed her husband and sons, and poisoned her spirit with anger, bitterness, and resentment towards God, but the Almighty still won. Naomi's dreams and hopes perished in the grave of adversity but God resurrected and restored everything beyond her expectations. He resurrected the dead dreams and fulfilled them in astonishing ways.

Naomi was told that God had not left her without a kinsman-redeemer. I want to tell you, you have a kinsman – redeemer. His name is Jesus Christ. He can redeem you from every situation and redeem all what you have lost in the adversities of life. Redemption and restoration is your right because you have a kinsman redeemer who has paid the complete price for your redemption and restoration.

Obed was not just a baby conceived because two people made love but he was a divine gift to bring renewal, sustenance, and restoration to the lives of Boaz, Ruth, and Naomi. God used the broken pieces of the lives of Boaz, Ruth, and Naomi to build a trophy of beauty and glory for the demonstration of the triumph of His plans and purposes not just for them but for mankind as a whole.

Ruth was already better than seven sons to Naomi but God decided to crown it with the beautiful trophy called Obed. That is what the God you serve can do. The God who brought restoration, renewal, and sustenance in the life of Naomi is your God.

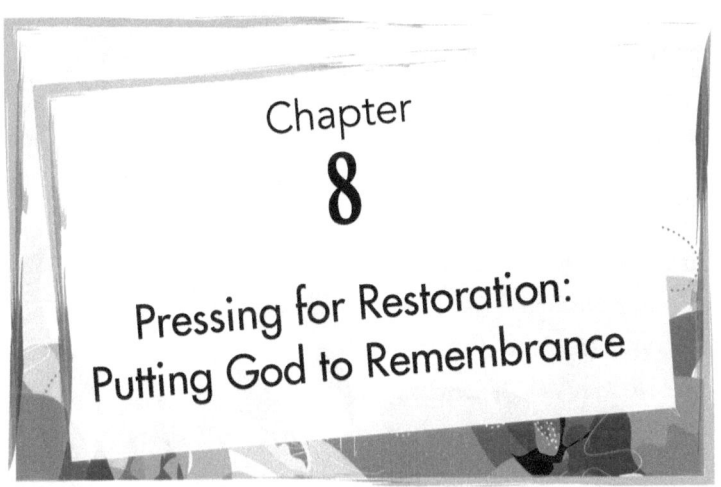

Chapter 8

Pressing for Restoration: Putting God to Remembrance

We did talk in chapter 2 of the pathway to restoration and listed nine aspects of that pathway to entering full restoration. In these closing chapters, I'll like us to discuss one other important aspect which has proven very useful and effective in ensuring you receive and enter full, total, and complete restoration.

After the necessary aspects on the pathway of restoration have been fulfilled as per the situation at hand, sometimes you will still have to press for restoration through the power of putting God to remembrance. There is tremendous power to initiate restoration when you put God to remembrance of His promise of restoration.

The book of Remembrance

There is a book of remembrance in the presence of our God kept as a tool for restoration. The Bible says,

> *16 Then those who feared the Lord talked with each other, and the Lord listened and heard. A scroll of remembrance was written in his presence concerning those who feared the Lord and honored his name.*
>
> *17 "On the day when I act," says the Lord Almighty, "they will be my treasured possession. I will spare them, just as a father has compassion and spares his son who serves him. 18 And you will again see the distinction between the righteous and the wicked, between those who serve God and those who do not.*

(Malachi 3:16-18)

There was a time in Israel when poverty, lack, sickness and diseases afflicted everybody. It was difficult to distinguish those who were under blessings and those who were under a curse. People had lost everything they had, especially those who served God, and it seemed the evil men and women remained untouched by the plague of lack and want. But then, God saw and heard all this and decided that a book of remembrance be written and kept in His presence for the day of restoration when He comes for His treasured possession.

The day of remembrance is the day for restoration of blessings and dignity. It is the day when God makes you to stand out from the crowd and distinguishes you as His favored one. The season of restoration is the time when God summons the angel in charge of the book of remembrance to open the book and read to Him. It is the time when God decides to remember His people to make them what they ought to be, and give them all that they lost.

We are in the day of remembrance

Because we are in the day of restoration, we are also in the day of remembrance. The Lord says, *"Put me in remembrance: let us plead together: declare thou, that thou mayest be justified"* (Isaiah 43:26, KJV). The Lord is commanding us to put Him to remembrance. He invites us to come into His Throne Room, the supreme court of the universe and plead our case for restoration. The Lord wants to acquit you of every charge of accusation from the enemy to keep you in bondage.

Whatever ground the devil is standing on to afflict, limit, or obstruct you shall be cut from under him in this day of remembrance and restoration. It is time to approach the throne of grace with boldness and confidence, by the blood of the Lamb of God, standing on the grounds of the New Covenant, and state our case for remembrance and restoration. By the reason of the blood, and our Advocate on high, our case shall prevail.

We have a better Covenant

David was someone who understood and made use of the power of putting God to remembrance. He understood that with remembrance comes restoration and often asked the Lord to remember him. In one such prayers he said,

> *"6 Remember, Lord, your great mercy and love, for they are from of old.7 Do not remember the sins of my youth and my rebellious ways; according to your love remember me, for you, Lord, are good."*
>
> (Psalm 25: 6-7)

David pleaded for remembrance and restoration on the grounds of God's mercy, goodness, and love. He pleaded with the Lord to forgive the sins of his youth and his rebellious ways, and remember him. Now, those of us in the New Covenant, have additional grounds on which to stand and ask for remembrance and restoration. We have the cross, the blood, and the empty tomb as additional grounds to approach the throne of grace and plead our case for remembrance and restoration.

In spite of your mistakes, errors, foolishness, or ignorance, you can still ask the Lord to remember and restore you on the grounds of His goodness, love, mercy, the blood, the cross, and the empty tomb.

Remember we said that prayer is one aspect of the pathway to restoration. You pray by pleading your case for remembrance and restoration in the court of the Most High. He said you should state your case for justification. And what better ground is there for justification than the finished work of the cross of Calvary? It is time to pray, *"Remember me oh God"*.

For the Sake of His Glory

Many times we as children of the King find ourselves in circumstances that contradict everything we have declared about our covenant relationship with the King, circumstances that reflect every contradiction to our statement of faith. And it is as such moments the enemy seizes every opportunity to mock our faith in, and allegiance to the King. Take a look at the following verses;

> *"2 Remember the nation you purchased long ago, the people of your inheritance, whom you redeemed — Mount Zion, where you dwelt…"18 Remember how the enemy has mocked you, Lord, how foolish people have reviled*

> *your name… "²²Rise up, O God, and defend your cause; remember how fools mock you all day long."*
>
> (Psalm 74: 2,18,22)

Three times in the same Psalm, the psalmist pleaded his case for remembrance and restoration. He pleaded with the Lord to remember them on the ground of redemption and the glory of the Lord which the enemy was mocking and reviling because of the circumstances that surrounded the nation. So it's time to tell the Lord that it's not about you but it's all about Him; His name, His glory, His cause, and His inheritance.

May be you have declared the goodness and generosity of your God and the power of His provision and now the enemy is mocking because you are in debt. May be you have declared the Lord as Jehovah Rapha who heals you and now you find yourself sick and the enemy is mocking your claims. It is time to ask the Lord to remember you and vindicate His Name.

You see, the Psalmist prayed again,

> *"⁵⁰ Remember, Lord, how your servant has been mocked, how I bear in my heart the taunts of all the nations, ⁵¹ the taunts with which your enemies, Lord, have mocked, with which they have mocked every step of your anointed one."*
>
> (Psalm 89:50-51)

Pressing for Restoration: Putting God to Remembrance 85

Beloved, it is time to ask the Lord to remember you and vindicate His name. You must understand that the Lord has made everything beautiful in its time. He has established seasons, and we are in the season, in the time of remembrance and restoration. So it's time for you to plead your case until restoration comes or assurance is given you that it is done.

Job said to the Lord, *"If only you would set me a time and then remember me!"* (Job 14:13b). He understood that there is a time for remembrance and didn't want that time to pass him by. The time God has set for your remembrance and restoration is now, behold the season, and press for complete restoration.

Chapter 9

When God Remembers You

In the last chapter we saw the need to press for restoration by putting God to remembrance. We saw the grounds on which we should make our requests and press our case for remembrance and restoration. In this chapter I will like us to look at what happens when God remembers you. Let's look at some examples of cases where people put God to remembrance and the results.

Noah

> *"But God remembered Noah and all the wild animals and the livestock that were with him in the ark, and he sent a wind over the earth, and the waters receded." (Genesis 8:1)*

May be like Noah you have experienced the destruction of things around you, may be like him you find yourself in the midst of flood waters that have lasted longer than you expected. May be you have been preserved from a calamity and the place God used for your preservation has become a place of discomfort. May be you have been drained physically, mentally, and emotional by the floodwaters in which you find yourself. You know you are where God wants you to be, doing what He wants you to do, yet your floodwaters have refused to recede.

In this season of remembrance and restoration, I see the Lord remembering you and causing your **floodwaters to recede.** I see Him driving back the storm and reversing the circumstances for your restoration. I see Him opening the door for you and letting you out into a place of **comfort and freshness** of air. You have been in discomfort for too long, you have endured for too long. It's time to come out.

Abraham

> *"So when God destroyed the cities of the plain, he remembered Abraham, and he brought Lot out of the catastrophe that overthrew the cities where Lot had lived."*

> (Genesis 19:29)

May be like Abraham you have loved ones who are in a rather dangerous and precarious situations and there is nothing you can do in your own power to ensure their safety and return. It may be a friend, sibling, child, parent, or distant relative for whose safety you have concern. As you put the Lord to remembrance in this season of restoration, like Lot, God is able to bring them out of the catastrophe, He is able to preserve their lives in the midst of calamity and bring them out unscathed.

Will you press for remembrance and restoration so that *"29 When people are brought low and you say, 'Lift them up!' then he will save the downcast. 30 He will deliver even one who is not innocent, who will be delivered through the cleanness of your hands."* (Job 22:29-30)? Yes! Now is the season, now is the time. May the Lord remember you and **preserve and deliver** your loved ones.

Rachel and Hannah

> *"Then God remembered Rachel; he listened to her and enabled her to conceive."*
>
> (Genesis 30:22)

> *"11 And she made a vow, saying, 'Lord Almighty, if you will only look on your servant's misery and remember me, and not forget your servant but give her a son, then I will give him to the Lord for all the days of his life, and no*

> *razor will ever be used on his head…' and the Lord remembered her.* [20] *So in the course of time Hannah became pregnant and gave birth to a son. She named him Samuel, saying, 'Because I asked the Lord for him.'"*
>
> (1 Samuel 1:11-20)

In this season of remembrance and restoration, there will be divine enabling for conception. Not just conception of babies but **conception of ideas, businesses, and inventions**. The womb of your spirit will be opened for pregnancy with vision and destiny. I see birthing of gifts, talents, ministries, and businesses in this season of remembrance and restoration.

Barrenness will be far removed from the midst of God's people as we press on for remembrance and restoration from ridicule and shame we have endured because of fruitlessness. I see you being restored to fruitfulness as you press for remembrance and restoration. As you draw in intimacy with the heavenly Bridegroom He will sow in you the seed of **destiny, vision, and purpose** so that in the course of time you may become pregnant and fulfill your divine destiny.

Joseph

In seasons of remembrance God causes men to remember, who ought to have remembered you, but who for some

When God Remembers You 91

reason forgot. And when God does it, it will be time for your **promotion and uplifting**. Seasons of remembrance are seasons of **establishment in high places**; they are seasons of elevation and exaltation by God. It is time to be fetched from the prison of bondage to the throne.

There are people whose hearts God will touch and remind them of the favor they need to show you. Somebody will mention your name in quarters of influence and decision. You remember Joseph and the cupbearer of Pharaoh? After Joseph had interpreted their dreams, he said to the cupbearer, *"14 But when all goes well with you, remember me and show me kindness; mention me to Pharaoh and get me out of this prison"* (Genesis 40:14). Unfortunately for Joseph, *"23 The chief cupbearer, however, did not remember Joseph; he forgot him"* (Genesis 40:23).

May be like Joseph, there are people you have rescued and assisted in the past who today are in high places but they have forgotten the goodness and kindness you showed them. In this season of remembrance and restoration the Holy Spirit will remind men of the favor they need to show you. He will touch the hearts of men and women who matter to mention your name to high quarters for **promotion and elevation.**

When the time for remembrance came for Joseph, it is written that the cupbearer was suddenly reminded of the favor shown him by Joseph and made mention of him to Pharaoh, who sent for him immediately. In the split of a second in the season of remembrance and restoration Joseph went from a dungeon to the palace in a position of leadership and authority. Only the Holy Spirit could bring Joseph into the mind of the cupbearer who had forgotten him. This is your season, press for remembrance.

The Israelites

When the Israelites were suffering in slavery to Egypt and cried out for deliverance, the Bible says, *"God heard their groaning and he remembered his covenant with Abraham, with Isaac and with Jacob"* (Exodus 2:24). It was a season of remembrance and through their groaning, they put God to remembrance. God showed up and said to Moses, *"⁵Moreover, I have heard the groaning of the Israelites, whom the Egyptians are enslaving, and I have remembered my covenant. ⁶ Therefore, say to the Israelites: 'I am the Lord, and I will bring you out from under the yoke of the Egyptians. I will free you from being slaves to them, and I will redeem you with an outstretched arm and with mighty acts of judgment."* (Exodus 6:5-6)

In this season of remembrance I see the Lord bringing you out from every bondage into the **glorious liberty** of the sons of God. I see your troubles in trouble because God has arisen on your behalf. Every yoke shall be broken in this season of remembrance and restoration. You will enjoy the benefits of divine concern. Your redemption is at hand, and total deliverance is yours.

Begin to celebrate your freedom and confound your captors. It is the season of restoration, and you are being restored into total freedom. Speak to everything of yours that seems to be in captivity and declare **freedom** for it in this season of remembrance and restoration.

Samson

Because of compromise with sin and indulgence, Samson found himself stripped of power and vision and made into a slave boy in the hands of the philistines. The great and fearful Samson had become an object of mockery and shame the philistines could play around with. The deliverer had become the captive, reduced to a mere ridicule through the laps of immorality. And the Bible says he was reduced from an anointed to an entertainer.

May be like Samson you find yourself stripped of the power and authority that was yours in the Kingdom. May be you find yourself stripped of the Spirits' anointing and captive to sin and indulgence. May be you too have been made into a mere ridicule in the hands of the forces of evil, the enemies of your soul. But that is not the end of the story. It is written that, *"Then Samson prayed to the Lord, 'Sovereign Lord, remember me. Please, God, strengthen me just once more, and let me with one blow get revenge on the Philistines for my two eyes.'"* (Judges 16:28)

In the midst of all his calamity, Samson asked the Lord to remember him. He pressed his case for remembrance and in the split of a second God answered his prayers. His strength was restored and he accomplish in his dying bed much more than he had done while still alive. God is indeed a God of remembrance and restoration.

You too can cry out for **revival**, like Samson you too can be revived again. You can receive the **power and anointing of the Holy Ghost** in your life in a new dimension that will make you accomplish what you couldn't accomplish before. Say, *"remember me oh God and revive me again."*

The above examples are just a few of what happens when God remembers you. We can continue with other examples like Hezekiah, Nehemiah, and Cornelius, who all experienced restoration because of the power of remembrance. So, press on for remembrance and restoration. It is your covenant right in Christ Jesus.

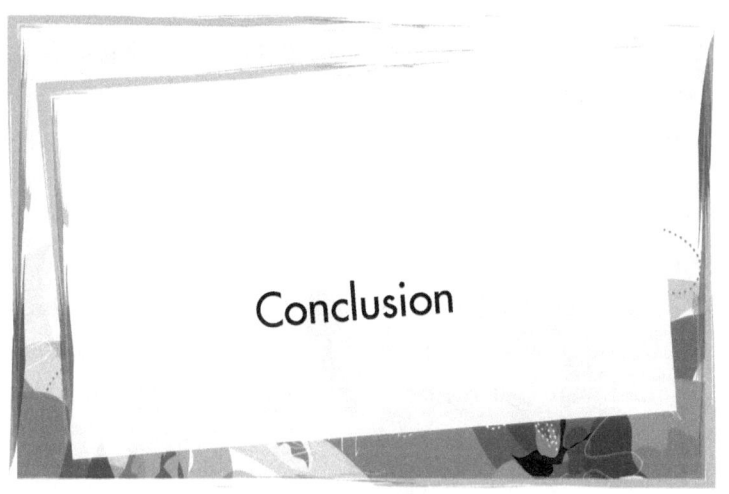

Conclusion

For there to be complete restoration in your life, you have to be committed to the Lord on His terms. The very first step to total restoration is to make the Lord Jesus your personal Lord and Savior. If there is sin in your life you will have to forsake it and turn completely and wholeheartedly to the Lord. May be you are not yet sure of your salvation. I want you to pray with me:

> *"Lord God almighty, I come to you today in the Name of Jesus and by His shed Blood. I ask you to forgive me for all the sins I have committed against You in attitude, motives, thoughts, words, and actions. I repent from all my sins and turn*

fully and wholly to You. Lord Jesus I embrace Your cross and from this day I take up my cross and follow You daily. Help me to live daily to please you in everything. In Jesus Name, amen."

If you just prayed that prayer sincerely, you are welcome to the kingdom of God and of His Christ. We will be delighted to help you grow in your life in Christ. Look for a local living church and become part of and serve the Lord where He plants you.

> To contact the author, write to
> E. C. Nakeli
> 40 S Church st.
> Westminster, MD 21157

www.ingramcontent.com/pod-product-compliance
Lightning Source LLC
Chambersburg PA
CBHW020659300426
44112CB00007B/452